THE LIFE & TIMES OF

REV. DR. PRESTON BLACKMON

THE MAN. THE MESSAGE. THE MISSION.

REV. SHEILA BLACKMON-NEAL

*Scriptures taken from NKJV unless otherwise noted.

Printed in the USA

ISBN:
978-0-578-78456-4 Hard Cover

Library of Congress Control Number:
2020908305

Authored by
Sheila Blackmon-Neal

Editor
Dr. Lakisha S. Forrester
Kingdom Builders Publications

Cover Design
LoMar Designs

Pictures
Personal Family Photo Library
Archives of Newspaper (Lancaster)

DEDICATION

First and foremost, I dedicate this book to my Heavenly Father, the everlasting God. He is the giver and sustainer of life and the giver of every perfect gift. He gifted me to be a teacher, preacher, writer, poet, songwriter, artist, singer, and worshipper. I am His child, and without Him, I am nothing. I am eternally grateful to God for my being.

To my loving mother, Wilma Myers Blackmon and my siblings: Krystal, the late Derrall Sr., Ricardo Sr., Denise, Andre, Charlene, Ada, Heath, the late Laritz, and LaShawn, God did this and I give Him glory, honor, and praise.

To Brandy, Sheena, Samuel, Shameka, LaToya, Antonio, Ashton, JaNya, Brayden, Carmen, and Preston, this is your keepsake!

Family, it's been twelve years since Dad's death; and with this book, we can rekindle his memory. So, this book is a forever treasure. Let me ask you to give me a solemn promise that you will read this book and it will be passed down to your children, your children's children, and to every generation beyond.

Lastly, to my earthly father, Rev. Dr. Preston Blackmon, who left an indelible mark on the hearts of so many citizens in the city and county of Lancaster, South Carolina, your story had to be told.

This is for you, Dad!

Table of Contents

ACKNOWLEDGMENTS

Without God's Holy Spirit leading and guiding me, this book wouldn't have been possible. I also believe His timing was ordained.

It was through Evangelist Sandra Harrell that I met Elder Louise Smith (both from Columbia, SC). At our first meeting, a loving friendship occurred among the three of us, not knowing it was a gateway to this blessed project honoring my dad, Rev. Dr. Preston Blackmon.

My dad meant so much to me; he was a blessed, gifted, and loving man. He was a man that accomplished a lot in his lifetime; a man I believe is worth honoring. I am eternally grateful for who he was, for what he did, and for the legacy he left us all in the city and county of Lancaster, South Carolina.

INTRODUCTION

What could be more gracious than a child receiving from the Heavenly Father a wonderful, loveable, and God-fearing father?

A father who is committed to his home, his occupation, and to his fellowman.

A father who is loyal, faithful, and trustworthy.

A father who loves God, His Word, and His Truth.

A father who preached and practiced what he believed, leading by example.

A father who demonstrated God's love.

A father who wasn't perfect, but fair.

A father who walked according to God's will and His way.

Truly, God has blessed and favored me as his child, the seventh child.

I am blessed beyond measure because this is the kind

of father he has been to me.

~ Sheila Blackmon-Neal

I am so grateful that on July 11, 1958, after 7 p.m., my dad was home when my mother went into labor. My mom told me that when I arrived, my siblings were in the other room playing. She asked my dad to sing to muffle my shrieking voice. God placed my dad there to clutch and grab me as I entered into this world. He caught me before I hit the floor. He was such a protector, and I thank him for that.

My dad taught my siblings and me how to stand in faith and in the will of God. He was a special dad who hesitated not to give us God's truth. He was the epitome of a great father! He was a father to the fatherless; a friend to the friendless; a brother to the brotherless. What a gift from God my dad was.

With this book, I wanted to pay my respects to him and give him the honor that he deserves. I knew his life had to be told to his grandchildren and his great-grandchildren. I want my nieces, nephews, grandnieces, and grandnephews, who were born after he died, to learn about and remember his life, his love, and his legacy. I also want them to know what a fantastic role model and mentor their granddaddy was. I want generations to come to know he was a man with a mission and a message that came from his lion-heart.

Dad left a legacy for my mom, my siblings, and me. I want my mom to be extremely proud of who he was and what he represented. I want my siblings to know with greater respect that we had an awesome dad! A Humanitarian. A Renaissance man.

As you read this book, I pray that you are blessed as you look into the world of my dad, Rev. Dr. Preston Blackmon, and get to know the life and times of the man that I (and so many others) knew. This is his story, told from my perspective from the things he left on record.

Here's to you, Dad!

PART I: THE MAN

A NOTABLE RESIDENT
Chapter One

Lancaster, South Carolina, was named after the House of Lancaster, which was one of the two royal families competing for England's throne in the Wars of the Roses that were fought in the fifteenth century. Lancaster is nicknamed the "Red Rose City." We fellow Lancastrians proudly celebrate our motto, "Forward Together, the Spirit of Lancaster!"[1]

Lancaster is the birthplace to many who have made their mark in history. Among those notables in the political arena was the nation's seventh president and the 114th governor of South Carolina. We had notables that dominated the sports arena, such as professional baseball and professional football players, along with a gold and silver medalist, track and field star.[2]

Another Lancastrian native was an astronaut that walked on the moon. In the entertainment industry, many danced to the doo-wop sounds of a lead singer and songwriter of a Rhythm and Blues (R & B) group. Many also tuned in to watch a famous television, film, and Broadway star that rose to stardom in the United States and in Europe.[2]

And then there was my dad, Preston Blackmon, who was a son, brother, husband, father, leader, preacher, Sunday School superintendent, real estate owner, brick masonry contractor, public school teacher, community activist, and servant. It took a lot of things in Dad's hands, such as determination, focus, patience, and endurance to fulfill these and many more incredible roles in his lifetime. Because of my dad, Lancaster is a better place to live and reside.

A MOSES
Chapter Two

Many years ago, God placed it on my heart that my dad was like His servant, Moses, whose life and actions were chronicled in the Book of Exodus. Moses was used mightily by God. God's people, the Israelites, had been in bondage for 430 years; but God had a plan to send Moses to Egypt to tell Pharaoh, the taskmaster, to let His people go.

Like Moses, my dad was a servant, deliverer, and a spokesman for the people of God. He was called to deliver his people—the citizens of Lancaster County to hope, pray, live an honest life, work an honest job, raise a family, and to give back and make contributions to society. He just didn't tell them; he simply demonstrated what he preached. He didn't just talk the talk; he walked the walk, giving his life for the lives of others. He used his hands, his heart, and his head with the wisdom that God gave him to make a difference in the lives of everyone he came in contact with.

My dad always had something positive and inspiring to say. He was a man with a mission and a message. He spoke for God. He lived for God. He had faith like Moses. He was a mighty man and my role model.

My dad was a Moses in his own time, in his own right. A leader for all people. A deliverer who brought many (black, white, rich, or poor) out of darkness to see a marvelous light, especially within themselves. He stood in the gap for all of mankind with his mission and his message.

Moses delivered the law for God's people; my dad delivered the law to the lawless, the illiterate, the uneducated, and gave it to them in a way they could understand, with justice and fairness. My dad saw oppression; he saw injustices. He saw and heard the cries of God's people.

Dad had a voice that spoke with conviction, a voice of authority. When he spoke, everyone would listen. He always had something to say! He was afraid of nothing.

He had such courage, such boldness, such gall to defend his people and challenge his enemies. He knew who his enemies were; he knew many odds were stacked against him everywhere he went. Many times, he went alone in the enemy's camp, and each time he came out victorious.

Dad believed like Moses. Stood like Moses. Carried out God's plan like Moses. Moses talked with God. He interceded for God. So did my dad. They both were called to do many things in their lives; they were leaders, servants, God's elect— dependable, trustworthy, and chosen to perform miraculous deeds for the Father.

When Moses got to the Red Sea, God told him to tell His people that the enemies they saw today, they will see no more" (**Exodus 14:13**). In **Exodus 14:21**, the Bible said, "Moses stretched out his rod over the sea; and the Lord caused the sea to go back by a strong east wind all that night, and made the sea into dry land, and the waters were divided." When he parted the Red Sea, God's people walked away from their enemies on that dry land and were now safe.

Moses had a rod; Dad had tools. Tools for justice. Tools for teaching. Tools for policing. Tools for building. Tools for training others. Tools for rearing eleven children. Tools for survival. Tools for success. Thank God, he left many facets of tools for his children, grands, great-grands, and generations to come.

My dad used whatever was in his hands to be a blessing to people. He was skilled at everything he did. He was a perfectionist! He believed there was but one way to do something, and that was to do it right! I can only imagine as a child what the first thing in his hand was. I think it probably may have been a stick that he could use to draw images and visions in the dirt of what he wanted to do as a child. No wonder my dad turned out to be an artist and a successful brick mason contractor and instructor, drawing images of furniture and blueprints to build houses, churches, funeral homes, and other structures.

Dad was certainly gifted and talented with those hands of his. He was always doing something, always busy crafting something, teaching something, or demonstrating something. He wasn't just a crafty artist; he was an inventor. He took table legs to make wall partitions. He used a piece of plywood to make a kitchen island. He took a piece of wire and fashioned it into a door latch. If he couldn't afford a tool that he needed, he would create it. He was very thrifty and conservative, not wasteful at all! He had such ingenuity about things, such wisdom.

My dad always kept a small, multipurpose pocketknife in his front pocket. One day, I asked him to purchase me a pair of bedroom shoes. Rather than doing so, he asked me to bring him a discarded pair of my shoes, and out came his knife. You guessed it! He made me newly fashioned bedroom shoes! I was simply amazed. Dad would take that same knife to carve an apple, then turn around and trim his fingernails. Yuck! That was my dad! Gotta love 'em.

My sister Denise told me that same knife saved Dad's life. On one occasion, he became ill as though he was having a stroke. He stopped talking, his mouth became twisted, and he began to swallow his tongue. Within a split second, he drew out his knife and quickly placed it in his mouth upon his tongue. That knife became a God-given tool. And my dad survived a stroke. It was nobody but the hand of God that kept him alive on that day.

Dad certainly tried his best to complete everything God called him to do. Many people in our community would come to my dad when they needed help. They would call "Mr. Preston" if their electrical power got cut off, if they were treated rudely, falsely accused, judged wrongly, lost their job, had a school bus situation, needed funds until the next paycheck, or couldn't find a lawyer. Mr. Preston was there to represent them.

He didn't hesitate to intercede for the citizens of Lancaster; he was never too busy to respond. He believed in them. He was just that kind of a person. Dad would make calls, set up visits, and went to see about the people of Lancaster. It didn't matter how large or small the problem became; their problem became his problem.

If he found someone who couldn't read, he would tell them to, *"Learn how to read. Go to college. Get an education. Don't settle for less. Submit your résumé . Keep trying. Don't give up. Be honest. Volunteer. Do a good job. Work on your character. Learn how to treat people. Treat people the way you want to be treated. Smile. Speak to people. Use your manners. Pray. Believe God."* He had a way of encouraging and giving instructions all at the same time. That was Mr. Preston!

It is believed that the rod that Moses used to show signs and wonders was passed down from one generation to another. It is my sincere hope, belief, and prayer that whatever my dad had in his hands were used to better the lives of others. This book about his life will be passed down from one generation to the next and hopefully inspire all those who read it to make a significant impact in their own lives and in the lives of others.

THE BEGINNING
Chapter Three

My dad was the third child of seven to be born through the union of Willie and Ada Duncan Blackmon on March 16, 1926. He had one sister (Margaret) and five brothers: James ("JC"), Belleree ("Newt"), James, Willie ("WL"), and the baby boy, Bobby.

Somewhere near Gay Street in Lancaster, South Carolina

My dad was born during the Depression era. He was taught mostly by his Mulatto mother, who was meek, humble, and had to deal with issues from both sides of her race. He was a special child with an outspoken nature. He had an eccentric tenacity to hate discrimination and question the lack of opportunities. At times, never knowing when to be quiet, he earned that special recognition from his father's backhand, belt, or broom.

Very little information is known about my dad before the age of thirteen except that he joined the First Washington Baptist Church on Pleasant Hill Street in Lancaster, South Carolina.

My dad came from a rich history of industrial men and women, teachers, and entrepreneurs. His great-granddad, Mack Blackmon, was born in 1848; his great grandmother, Emma Blackmon, was born in 1849. They came from slavery to prosperity; they were real estate owners and farmers who had many workers assisting them. No wonder Dad had such great work ethics with a sense of pride and dignity about his work and what he owned; it came from his grandpa Mack.

William Mack & Emma Blackmon

His forefathers were not just industrious or prosperous; they loved God and their fellowmen. They had many workers and helped many slaves with their harvest from farming in their fields. Grandpa Mack helped organize and support the Pleasant Grove Missionary Baptist Church by donating land for its dwelling. This church is still standing and thriving today in the Primus Community, south of the city of Lancaster, where African Americans worship weekly. Who would have ever thought my dad would co-pastor at "The Grove" before God called him home? That was the favor of God evident in his life.

For many years, it was said that Grandpa Mack and Emma gave much of their earnings and resources to that same community. Their leadership was a moving force of great benefit in making life better for many people. Their lives were one of achievement and excellence, giving employment opportunities to many farmers by supplying funds, materials, and supplies.

Grandpa Mack labored long hours in the fields, while Emma worked endless hours caring for their thirteen children and spinning yarn to make their clothes. God blessed them and they prospered, leaving behind 614 acres of land. The land was divided among their thirteen children, leaving fifty acres and $1,000 in cash to each of them. Grandpa Mack passed on September 21, 1928, at the age of 80; Emma passed on July 15, 1955, at the age of 106. What a legacy they left!

My dad's heritage is represented by an oak tree which is a historical symbol that represents the Blackmon family's deep roots, spiritual growth, success, love, and strength. It is still standing in Grandpa Mack and Emma's yard off of Bypass #9 in Lancaster, South Carolina. In fact, our first family reunion in the late 1960's began in the same yard where the oak tree stood.

I can remember as a teenager, the tents, and several grills firing at the same time with all of our relatives enjoying the laughter, the music, and the dancing. Family was always important to my dad. He loved family gatherings and outings. He spearheaded and organized the Blackmon's Family Reunions when he could. Dad was always happy and excited to see his relatives back home on the "homeplace."

He was always a cheerful man of faith and had pride when it came to family. In each of our family reunion booklets is a picture of the oak tree; it continues to serve as a witness of inspiration to the many generations to come.

This tree still grows on the homeplace of Mack and Emma Blackmon. May it be a symbol of strength for our family.

THE PROUD SERVICEMAN
Chapter Four

While in the tenth grade, at the age of eighteen, my dad was drafted into the United States Air Force, serving as a tail gunner. After serving two years in World War II (1944-1946), Dad received an honorable discharge with the rank of corporal.

After his service, Dad returned to Lancaster, South Carolina, to graduate at the age of 21. He received his high school diploma on May 30, 1947, from the Lancaster Training School at Barr Street High School with a certificate in brick masonry.

One year later, he met the love of his life, Wilma Myers. On May 1, 1948, they became husband and wife and resided on Miller Street in Lancaster, South Carolina.

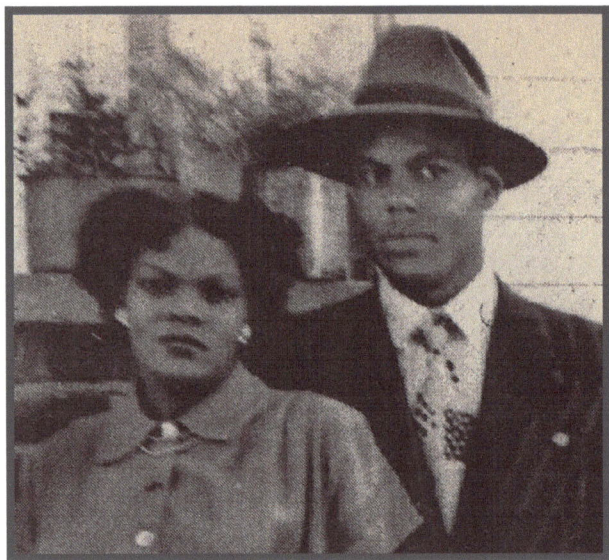

Jobs as a skilled master bricklayer in the South were scarce. When he couldn't find work, he would head to Detroit, New Jersey, and Chicago. After the jobs were completed, he would return home and stay close to his wife and children.

From the South to the North, from the North and back to the South, my dad never gave up. He had such perseverance, faith, and strength. Married with six children in 1959, after having worked for 10 years, when bricklaying became slow, this thin mustache, good-looking man who kept a smile on his face began to look for something different. He changed careers and became a police officer. He patrolled part-time on weekends from 4:00 p.m. to midnight.

Dad said that when he left the service, he had no intentions to return back to the South because of discrimination. "You can't run and fight at the same time" is what he was once told. I believe that statement motivated him to become a leader and a fighter in the downtown colored district of Lancaster as the first black officer (1960-1963). Officer Preston Blackmon made history!

These are dad's own words about policing. These words were recorded and printed in 2006 by Mr. Johnathan C. Ryan, a Staff Writer for the Lancaster News.

"Being the first black cop was very difficult. I faced constant adversity. It was a disturbing time to be a black man, much less a cop. You know, I never even drove a car the whole time I was on the force. I had to patrol by foot, covering Dunlap to White Streets, up to the community called the "Hill." There, I would have to keep the peace, protect, and serve.

If someone was drunk, I wouldn't snatch them. They knew they were drunk. I would talk to them and try to help them. While others seemed to be roughing them up, I just simply talked to them and gave simple advice. I think my pleasant and fair demeanor gained me more respect. It was my aim to be a gentleman in the community that I patrolled. A badge didn't give you the right to beat and curse and treat people like dogs. I treated people the way I wanted to be treated.

My first year, all I had was a .38-caliber pistol and a headstick. The second year, they put a phone in the middle of my beat. But at times, that didn't do much good. I had friends who told me they were at the police station when I'd call in needing help, and nobody was ever in a hurry to help or assist me. I had handcuffs and a gun, but no training; other than being instructed not to walk a detainee on my gun side. I was never assisted by other officers. They left me alone on my beat.

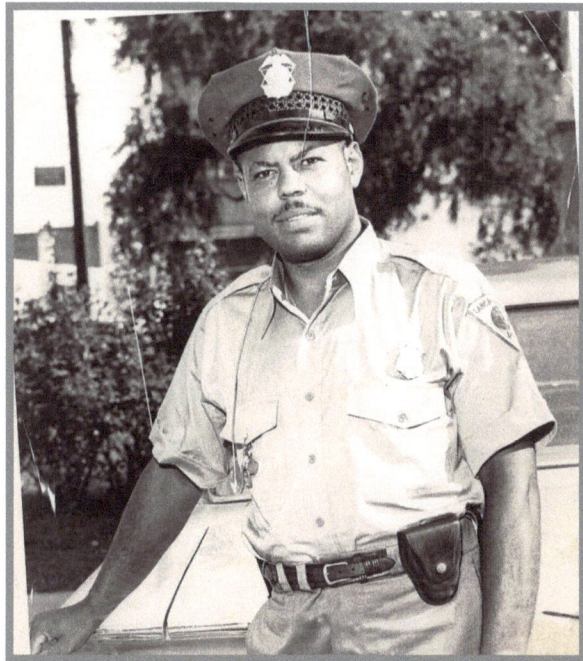

I never had any intention or idea to be a policeman; it was rough and I couldn't hardly get down some of the streets. You either had to have a lot of faith or be a crazy one and I depended solely on the Lord to guide and protect them. Many nights, I thought I wouldn't make it home. I talked too much and challenged the system; complicating my relationships with other officers. But I didn't let my actions and my words get me down. I took refuge in God, my family, and a sense of right and wrong. My Christian faith comforted me; providing a calm I need to serve.

As a police officer, I tried to be honest and fair; I never lost my cool. I remember what Joe Louis once said, 'If you lose your cool, you will lose the fight.' I never changed, I was always, the same Preston. If I had to die out there on the streets for my people, then so be it; I will risk my life to make a difference. This is the person I want the world to know."

Sheila's Perspective and Her Dad's Conversations

One day, the police chief insisted that Dad could not write any tickets or arrest any of the white race. Not even a parking ticket. He said to the chief, "If I can't write a ticket for both blacks and whites, I won't write them at all." He felt alone and isolated with no other policeman to work with. All Dad wanted to do was represent the community of Southside. He wanted them to know that by simply being there, he was protecting and keeping the peace for them. After three and half years, Dad had enough. He left the department in 1962 and didn't look back.

Dad said, "Someone has to be a pioneer and stand up for what's right and not worry about the cost. It's not easy and it takes something from deep down inside you to do that. I didn't think I could, but I did. It makes me feel proud to see a minority officer drive a police car. I never got to."

To take such discrimination and survive in spite of, Dad had to have been chosen. Chosen to serve. Chosen to lead. My dad was a Moses. He told me once, "If you are chosen, no one can prevent you." I am thankful Dad answered the call, and grateful that God chose him.

A MAN FOR SOUTHSIDE
Chapter Five

My dad wasn't a perfect man, but he was just, fair, fearless, courageous, and astute. He was an educator, an innovator, a creator, and a builder. He was one person to one and someone else to another. He was an advisor, a counselor, a shoulder to lean on, and a listening ear. I can go on and on. His mission was to help any and every one that needed help. His message was to keep the faith and have hope and trust in God.

God turned his scars into stars; stars that shone brightly to the heart of many souls, especially in the Southside Community.

There in Southside, the east side of Lancaster, you could always find my dad ministering to a bewildered girl or to a distraught boy who needed directions, a smile, or assurance that everything would be alright. That was the kind of person he was. He spoke as an apostle, prophesied as a prophet, and was a servant and friend to all.

PART II: THE MESSAGE

A MESSENGER FROM GOD
Chapter Six

Dad had so many notes. So many pads. This was taken from one of them.

The Word of God in Alphabet

A. **Almighty**. Exodus 6:3. I *am* the LORD. I appeared to Abraham as God Almighty, *by* My name LORD.
B. **Beginning**. Revelation 1:8. I am the Beginning.
C. **Corner Stone**. 1 Peter 2:5. The living stone.
D. **Deliverer**. Daniel 3:17. God is able and will deliver us.
E. **Eternal Life**. John 10:28. I give unto my sheep eternal life.
F. **Food**. Psalm 136:25. He giveth food to all flesh.
G. **Good**. Psalm 25:8. Good and upright is the Lord.
H. **Heaven**. Psalm 119:89. The Word is settled in heaven.
I. **Immortal**. 1 Timothy 1:17. Now unto the King eternal, immortal, invisible. The only wise God. Be honor and glory forever endureth.
J. **Joy**. Nehemiah 8:10. For the joy of the Lord is your strength.
K. **King**. Psalm 10:16. My King and my God.
L. **Love**. 1 John 4:7. Love is of God.
M. **Master**. Matthew 23:8. One is your Master, even Christ.
N. **Near**. Matthew 24:33. He is near, even at the door.
O. **Omnipotent**. Revelation 19:6. The Lord God; Omnipotent reigned.
P. **Powerful**. Psalm 29:4. The voice of God is powerful.
Q. **Quick**. Hebrews 4:12. The Word of God is quick.
R. **Righteous**. John 11:25. Resurrection and Life.
S. **Son of God**. John 1:49. Son of the Most High.
T. **Truth**. John 1:14. He is Grace and Truth.
U. **Unwavering Love**. John 3:16. For God is Love.
V. **Victorious**. 1 Corinthians 15:57. We are victorious through our Lord Jesus Christ.
W. **Wonderful**. Isaiah 9:6. Our Emmanuel as Counselor.
X. **X-cellent**. Psalm 8:1. Excellent in all the earth.
Y. **Yearned**. Romans 8:26. Yearned over by the Holy Spirit.
Z. **Zealous**. Titus 2:14. For every good work.

Dad became a changed person when he testified it was God who saved him and put him on a street called "Straight." He was a faithful praying man; a singing church man. He loved his God, his family, and his church. I heard him say to me, "I finally got it right with the Lord." Not only was my dad like Moses, but he was like King David, a man after God's own heart.

Oftentimes, my dad, mom, and six or seven of us would ride in a station wagon to First Washington Baptist Church in Lancaster, South Carolina, where he served in many capacities.

Dad was the superintendent for Sunday School, but he was also active on the deacon board and choir. He was a teacher, a helper, and a giver. If anyone needed anything done in the community or church, he was dependable.

First Washington Baptist Church
Established 1890

TRUSTEE BOARD

From left: Joe Asgill, Willie D. Cureton, Columbus Parker, Franklin P. Barnes Chairman: Theodore Montgomery and inset, A. R. Rucker. Absent from picture are Cicero Seegars, Leonard W. George and Alonzo Robinson.

DEACON BOARD

From left: Robert Reed, Preston Blackmon, C. N. Wilson, Chairman; George Witherspoon, Robert Truesdale, W. J. Gordon, D. B. Bailey, Robert Ford. Absent from picture are Harrison Cunningham and J. W. Blackmon.

BAPTIST TRAINING UNION

From left, front row: Marsha Gordon, Stephonne Smith, Cathy Catoe, Robin Duren, Miss Shirnetha Robinson, Mazzie Wilson, Miles Smith, Jr., Second row: Mrs. Carrie B. Massey, Mrs. Almetta Blackmon, Miss Gayle Gordon, Miss Donna Smith, Miss Pamala Smith. Third row: Rev. Miles O. Smith, Mrs. Roberta Stewart, Mrs. Hattie Gamble, Mrs. Mandy Robinson, Mrs. Bessie Hilton and Mrs. Inez Clinton. Back row: C. N. Wilson, Charles Gordon, Willie Gordon and Mr. Preston Blackmon, President.

SENIOR CHOIR

Front row: Miss Janie McCrory, Mrs. Johnnie M. Adams, Mrs. Margaret Boykin, Mrs. Polly C. Jackson, Miss Mildred F. Robinson, Mrs. Janie Cunningham and Miss Gayle Gordon, Pianist. Back row: Mr. Preston Blackmon, Mrs. Julia Segers, Mrs. Janie Duncan, Mrs. Irene Stewart, Mrs. Gertrude Stuckey, Mrs. Carrie Massey, Mrs. Carol Parker, Organist and Mr. Willie Gordon, Sr., President.

I have fond memories of being at the breakfast table after dad finished cooking grits and biscuits. He would pray and listen to Mahalia Jackson, Shirley Caesar and the Caravans, and Reverend Dr. James Cleveland. Those gospel legends meant a lot to him. Their song lyrics built his faith, gave him courage when times were hard, and strengthened his belief in God. Dad didn't find it robbery to sing along with them!

Our house was a shrine that housed and reverence the Word of God. In addition to the gospel tapes and albums, he always had one or two Bibles in the living room and in his bedroom. He had a host of religious literature in sight, from books on faith, books by Kenneth Copeland, Bible study pamphlets, and Crisis magazines.

Whenever anyone stopped by our home, it didn't matter who it was; Dad always had a Word from the Lord to share. I felt God pulling on Dad. I sensed his testimony and his witness were changing him for the better.

After he accepted the call of God, by the leading of the Holy Spirit, he left First Washington Baptist Church after spending nearly 50 years there. God was "up to something." And so it happened, in the fall of 1982, my dad began to preach. It was no surprise; I knew my dad would eventually preach the gospel. I was so happy when he accepted the call, because he ran from God so many years. I'm so thankful to God for his faithfulness and the mercy He bestowed upon my dad.

Dad preached his first sermon at the Mount Sinai Fire-Baptized Holiness Church on Brooklyn Avenue in Lancaster, South Carolina. His overseer was Bishop Bowens.

Dad was on fire. He loved God! He was real!

With such fire from God leading and guiding my dad to "all" truths, he began to instill godly values in our home, in our community, in our church, and throughout his life.

After his ordination, he began pastoring at Bowens Chapel Holiness Church in Wadesboro, North Carolina. There, his pastorate lasted two years; and soon, he was moved to St. John Holiness Church in Pageland, South Carolina.

To show himself approved unto God, Dad enrolled in the Atlanta Bible College in Rock Hill, South Carolina. He also took biblical classes at the University of South Carolina to further his study as a preacher. My dad was on a mission, with a message from God to teach and preach the gospel to the masses.

His other religious affiliations included being an outreach minister at White Oak Manor Nursing Home, Lancaster Rehabilitation Center, Springs Memorial Hospital, and the Prison Ministry.

His last assignment as a minister of the gospel was at Pleasant Grove Missionary Baptist Church in Lancaster, South Carolina. There, he was an Associate Minister and assisted Reverend Otis Lathan. It's interesting to note that Dad finished his course on earth there. This church was in the Rich Hill Community; it was actually built on land donated by his great-grandfather Deacon Mack Blackmon and his wife Emma, the first church mother. Ain't God a good God?

The three of them are buried at this church, a stone's throw away from each other. It is my wish that each generation of my family would take time to visit their graves.

On September 14, 2003, Dad was honored by C. E. Graham Bible College & Seminary with an Honorary Doctor of Christian Humanitarian Service degree. The school thought he was deserving because of all the things he had done for the city and county of Lancaster, South Carolina.

THE SERMON WRITER
Chapter Seven

Actual Sermonic Excerpt:

From the Desk of

Rev. Dr. Preston Blackmon

We are his workmanship, created
in Christ Jesus

The work of God in the earth
presents, from age to age, a
striking similarity in every refor-
mation or religious movement. The
principles of God's dealing with
men are ever the same. The
important movement of the present
have their parallel in those of the
past, and the experience of the
church in former ages has lessons
of great value for our own time
No truth is more clearly taught
in the Bible than that God by
His Holy Spirit especially directs His
servants on earth in the great move-
ments for the carrying forward of
the work of salvation. Men are
instruments in the hand of God,
employed by Him to accomplish
His purposes of grace and mercy.
Each has his part to act, to
each is granted a measure of
light, adapted to the necessities
of his time, and sufficient to
enable him to perform the
work which God has given him
to do.

But no man, however honored of Heaven, has ever attained to a full understanding of the great plan of redemption, or even to a ~~perfect~~ perfect appreciation of the divine purpose in the work for his own time. Men do not fully understand what God would accomplish by the work which He gives them to do. They do not comprehend, in all its bearings, the message which they utter in His name.

I. Born again, (John 3: of the Spirit — (Born from above)

II. Born of the water

Save us — includes delivering us from error
B — restoring to health
C — healing

Jesus — I am saying to you, unless anyone be born from above (from heaven, again, anew, from the first) he is not able to see (discover to experience — to know the Kingdom of God.

Nicodemus say to Him "How (in what manner, by what means) is a man able to be born, being an old man)

Nes is not able to enter into the womb of his mother a second time and be born (is he)?

5v Jesus answer Certainly, certainly I am saying to you, except anyone be born from out of water (that which refreshes the soul) and from out of spirit (the vital principle) he is not able to enter (at any time) into the Kingdom of the (one true) God.

v6 - The (child) having been born out of flesh is flesh, and the (child) having been born out of the spirit is spirit (is activated by the spirit)

The spirit breathes (given immortality and spiritual gifts) where (the spirit) wills, and and you are hearing the voice (of the spirit) but you are not knowing from where (the spirit) comes and where (the spirit) goes so is everyone having been born from out of the spirit

Page 4

THE TEACHER
Chapter Eight

Dad had his hands in so many things, from preaching the good book (the Bible) to his masonry credentials. On any given day, he would have his favorite pocketknife, books, a Bible, hammer, masonry tools, pencils, pens, and/or paper either in his hands or sticking out of his pockets. What my dad used in his hands, depicted his life.

After eight years of laying bricks, he became his own brick masonry contractor. He did so for over 35 years. After his health became a challenge at the age of 47, Dad decided to stretch himself and go back to school to further his education. He always wanted to strive for more. Obtain more. Learn more. He knew to get further ahead in life, it was going to take more; and he accepted the challenge.

He had the desire to teach others how to become master bricklayers. So, in 1966, he enrolled in South Carolina State College in Orangeburg, South Carolina, to become a certified teacher to teach masonry; he received an Industrial Arts degree.

He was a firm believer that you can't run from the problems of life, you have to educate yourself and challenge it. And that he did.

His first teaching assignment was in Buford, Georgia. He would work there all week and come home on the weekends. The drive was nearly four hours. What a sacrifice!

His second assignment as an Industrial Teacher was at the Aiken County Vocational Training School in Aiken, South Carolina (1969-1970).

His third assignment was at Barr Street High School. He taught disadvantaged and handicapped students. And lastly, also in Rock Hill, South Carolina, he taught at

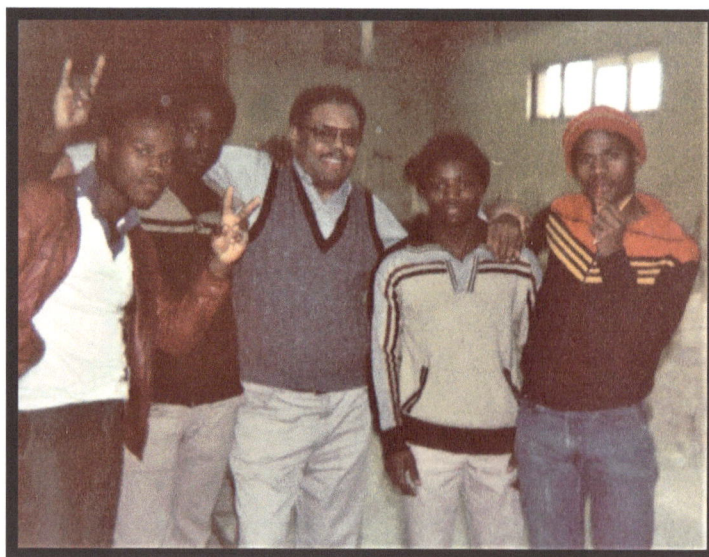

York County Career Development Center until he retired in 1988.

Whether he was in and out of the classroom, up and down Hampton Road, in the bank, at the mall, or near the post office—it didn't matter to my dad; he always had a voice for the people.

PART III: THE MISSION

THE MISSIONARY & SERVANT
Chapter Nine

From being a preacher, to a teacher, to a leader to the people, the public, the city, and the county of Lancaster, my dad was always on a mission! Whatever he found his hands to do, he did it! Justice was in his hand, law and order in his head, coupled with community action, peace, and unity among the people in his heart. My dad became a public city leader, a community leader, and committed servant. He always volunteered his services in many facets. All he wanted to do was make a difference.

If working nearly 10 hours a day wasn't enough, my dad found time to mentor, volunteer, help organize, and/or become a member of several committees, organizations, and boards. Below are some of his most notable contributions:

- Advisory Board member to the Lancaster County School District community-in-schools
- Served on committees to raise funds for the Lancaster Youth Center
- 3rd Vice President of the NAACP (lifetime member with over 50 years)
- Member of the South Carolina Black Caucus
- President and Vice President of the Lancaster Ministerial Association
- South Carolina Municipal Legislative Board
- Member of The American Legion, Post 31
- Member of the Lancaster Disabilities and Special Needs Board of the Lancaster Board of Education
- Chairman of the Emergency Aid Act Advisory Board of the Lancaster Board of Education
- 2002 Father of the Year Award; King David Masonic Lodge
- 1st Black Volunteer Clergy Staff for the Marion Sims Hospital
- 1st Black Policeman for Lancaster County
- 1st Black Constable in the Gills Creek Township for Lancaster County
- Longest running term for City Council (34years)/ Mayor Pro Tempore (pro tem)
- Habitat for Humanity community projects
- The Southside Crime Watch Group

- Board member for the Southside Literary Project under the direction of Apostle George and Pastor Stella Williams
- Faithful member of the Southside Kidz Club
- Mentor for the Adopt-A-Leader Program
- Initiated and helped organized the construction for the Southside playground

In his honor, the Southside playground, in which he helped organize, was renamed Preston Blackmon Park in 2010. It's a beautiful park sitting on seven acres of land. It is located at 500 Conner Street and includes a children's playground, a slide, a swing set, two picnic shelters, restrooms, two basketball courts, and one softball field on seven acres of land. What a proud place to visit!

With so many contributions in the Southside Community, the Family Literary Success Center on Palmetto Street was renamed The Preston Blackmon Family Success Center in Lancaster, South Carolina. This center serves individuals who are interested in literacy, obtaining a GED, family skills, parenting classes, among a host of other programs to serve the people. Many individuals come to brush up on their computer skills. It is under the direction of Apostle George and Pastor Stella Williams. My family and I are indebted to their vision of hard work and commitment to the success of this center. Presently, the center is undergoing renovations to improve the lives of the community for generations to come.

To learn more about the center, visit http://prestonblackmoncenter.org

On February 7, 2007, Congressman John Spratt, Jr. awarded my dad a certificate of Special Congressional Recognition for District #5 for all of the services he rendered in his lifetime. Congressman Spratt declared March 3, 2003 to

be "Preston Blackmon Day" for the city of Lancaster, South Carolina. Last, but not least, President George W. Bush honored my dad's memory with a certificate of recognition for his devoted and selfless service in the United States Armed Services.

My dad, whatever and wherever he placed his head, hand, and heart, success soon followed. He was dedicated and faithful to all the citizens of Lancaster. My dad once said, "In the righteousness of God, you can do anything. If you love people, God will support you in every effort and advancement. The Bible says, God is love. Don't say you love me and not show it. It's an action word."

I am so proud of my dad. What a mighty man of valor, strength, honor, and dignity. He held many offices, received numerous awards and certificates, but didn't like accolades. He was a humble man, a Moses, but never boasted about any of his successes or accomplishments; he only boasted in the Lord **(Jeremiah 9:23-24)**.

He gave all the glory to God. When I would say, "Thank you, Dad," he would respond by saying, "Don't thank me, thank God!"

THE BUILDER
Chapter Ten

I remember so many Monday mornings watching Dad roll out of the yard with his green Chevy truck and his cement mixer bolted behind it. I can still hear our dog, Buster, barking and chasing him as he sped out of the driveway to return late that same evening. He loved his work. He took pride in everything he built and owned. He built our home in 1963 or 64 on Hampton Road. We were proud of that home, not only because it housed our family, but knowing that Dad built it with his own hands made it even more special.

Dad was such a hard worker; he didn't play when it came down to work. My brother Andre told me that dad could hardly keep a crew with him. He outworked his helpers, two to one! He laid nearly 1,500 bricks on any given day. The bricks would come in stacks of 500 and he would nearly complete three stacks by the end of his day. My baby brother Heath recalled getting hit in the head by flying bricks. Dad would throw at least two or three at one time to keep the job flowing.

Dad contracted and subcontracted a lot of structures in and around Lancaster County, but I could only remember a few. He built Crawford's Funeral Home on Meeting Street, the Lancaster High School Band Room, and the First Washington Baptist Church. First Washington was our home church. Dad was there over fifty years. He took pride in knowing that he built our church.

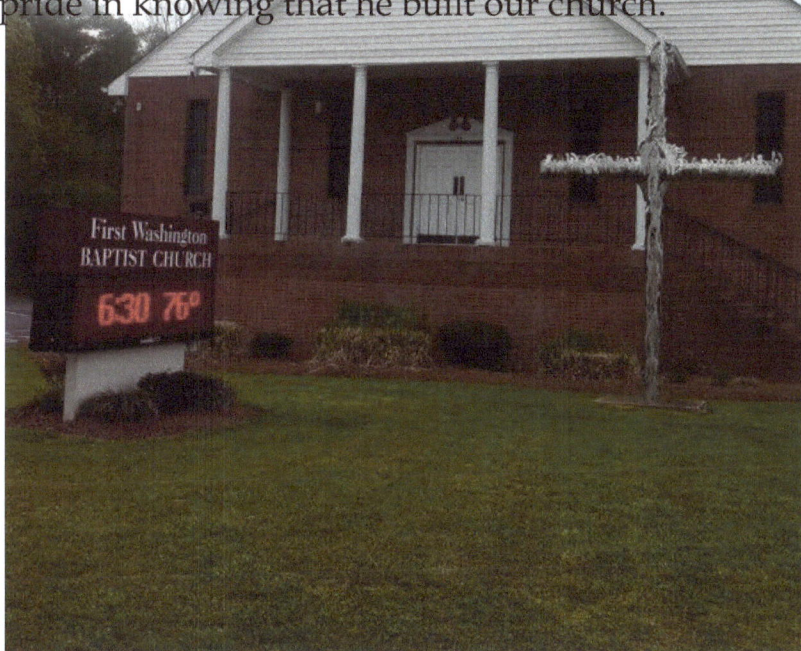

6-18-8¢

Staff Photograph by Jeff Zahr

Preston Blackmon and his son, Heath, put up a new welcome sign in front of the First Washington Baptist Church on Barr Street Thursday.

The father and son team spent about eight hours a day from June 11 to June 16 putting up the new sign. Temperatures were consistently in the 90's throughout the week.

Blackmon, member of the Lancaster City Council, teaches brick masonry at the Career Development Center in Rock Hill, and Heath is a rising senior at Lancaster High School.

Dad had a vision to leave each of his nine children a home. He was an astute businessman, buying and managing nine homes. He left land in Twin Pines, homes and land in Southside, and off Pageland Highway Bypass #9. He was truly blessed and highly favored by God.

My dad and mom raised 10 children, worked daily, volunteered in the community, and were servants in the church. My dad was a leader among the people, managed his home and nine others, worked in and out of town laying bricks, and then became a preacher, a laborer of the gospel. This man was truly a renaissance man.

No wonder he was a man of faith, prayer, and believed in the Word of God. He honored his God in everything. He gave his God the glory. For dad truly believed that without God, he could do nothing.

BEING "PRESTON"
Chapter Eleven

When I moved back to South Carolina in November of 2018 after being away from home thirty-three years, the Spirit of God impressed upon me to write this book. It was so much to be told to the next generations who missed the life, love, the laughter, and the legacy of my dad. After much prayer and meditation, the title of the book came to me as well.

After I got settled in January of 2019, I heard the voice of God again. "Write the book!" He said. So, I sat down and wrote down a list of items I knew I would need to get started. With much prayer and supplication, I asked God, "Where do I begin? Where do I obtain information about his life, his childhood, his siblings, and his religious and community affiliations?" I began to petition the Lord. "Lord, I need newspaper clippings, documents, résumés, photos, and to make phone calls. Lord, is this really you?" And lo and behold, within three to four months, God provided everything that I needed for this project; I was able to check off everything from my list. I found it all! With God's confirmation, I knew He was in it.

The more I read about my dad, the more I wanted to know. The more I wanted to delve right into his mind and his thoughts. Every time I would find a piece of information about him in our home, I wanted to know: What made him tick? What made him a strong-willed person? What motivated him? Who was his role model? Where did he get such a drive? Such vision? What did he do in his spare time? What did he like? Dislike? How did he stay sane with so many responsibilities, commitments, meetings, jobs, hats to wear, children to raise, and see about himself?

Every chance I got, I would go to Mom's house and begin to dig and search meticulously. I would make sure she wasn't looking and dove right into Dad's file cabinet that was still intact on our back porch. I found a wealth of information, including old newspaper clippings and articles that involved Dad. My, my; this man didn't throw anything away is what I thought. He saved everything! Mom used to fuss all the time about trying to find enough space for "his stuff."

He even built bookshelves in the rear bedroom and downstairs in the den to accommodate all of his belongings. It was unbelievable that a man who struggled to read as a young adult, developed a desire and love for reading. But, that was my dad. He valued education. He knew that reading had to be the principle thing to be successful in life.

In my search, I found my 5th grade report card, a poem I wrote in the 6th grade, my grant papers from 1975 when I applied for college, along with my sisters' college Basic Educational Opportunity Grant (BEOG) applications from 1972. He kept our school record pictures, report cards from each of us, copies of financial loans, and receipts from tenants, insurance, and tax information. You name it, he had it!

I saw my basketball photo from 1973. I saw old photos

The Lancaster Lady Bruins have yet to win a game this season, but coach John Dodson believes his team has improved greatly over the past few games. Players pictured are: Kneeling: Ann Paul, Maxine Crockett, Terry Williams, Sheila Blackmon, and Pamela White. Back row: Rita Tripp, Lisa Cowan, Mirriam Webb, Jan Wright, Marilyn Tillman, and Robin Bumgardner.

of his children and grandchildren. I saw a picture of Dad and Heath, Andre's third son's 5th grade picture, and Dad's three oldest grands. Oh boy, did he love his grands! He saved pictures of all of his cousins, his brothers, and sister. He just loved people!

In his file cabinet, I found CDs and DVDs of different pastors' recorded sermons, especially his beloved pastor, Reverend Otis Latham. He collected coins, family reunion books, and pictures.

He saved receipts from purchases. He had biblical pamphlets and bank books. Dad saved all of his city notes and packets from meetings. He was a stickler for record keeping.

I even found a letter dated in the 1960's where the bank denied giving him a loan to purchase our home. There was a note written on it that said, "I want my children to have a copy of this letter." God made a way somehow and our home was built.

It was evident that Dad had great faith in God.

He loved black history. He had newspaper articles of men and women of color who made contributions from many different states. He had clippings of individuals who received awards in science, education, and music; people of color who had made history as the first female police chief, the first black astronauts, and the first black Miss Lancaster. He was always interested in seeing the African American race grow and flourish.

Awarded NAACP Plaques

Edward Francis, associate executive director of the South Carolina Democratic Party (left, front row), was the guest speaker at the annual Freedom Awards Banquet of the Lancaster Branch of the NAACP on Sunday. Awards were presented to several members for their contribution of service to the county. Above are, from the left, front row: Francis; Dr. D. A. Rucker, first Black to serve on County Board of Education; Fred Thomas, first Black elected to City Council; Baxter Mackey, treasurer, local chapter. Back row, Elton Truesdale, membership chairman; Preston Blackmon, first Black on Lancaster Police Dept.; Dr. J. A. Boykin, toastmaster at banquet; and Tommy Walker, first Black deputy sheriff. Other awards were presented to Deputy Jimmy Brown and Dr. J. J. Clinton, long-time Lancaster physician and a past president of NAACP. (Staff photo by Mike Slade)

It made him proud to see how far we have come since the Reconstruction era.

I saw articles on the deaths of President John F. Kennedy and Ronald Reagan. He even had an article on Rev. Dr. Martin Luther King, Jr. delivering his "I Have a Dream" speech. He kept articles on local prominent blacks he was close to, such as Mr. Gonzie Lee Twitty, Reverend Emily McIlwain, Mr. A.R. Rucker, Mr. Tommy Walker, Reverend Mifflin Smith, Dr. James Boykin, Ms. Birda Mackey, Mr. T. J. Witherspoon, and Sergeant James Jones.

He kept clippings that highlighted local sorority and fraternity friends, Barr Street High School's Class of 1941, the Gills Creek Dam Project, the N.A.A.C.P., nuclear weapons, local school crossing guards, Miss Black America, "Here and There" columns from the Lancaster News, earthquakes in Turkey, the Lancaster County Board of Commission, Senator Strom Thurman, and Reverend Jesse Jackson.

He was particularly interested in social injustices, locally and nationally. For example, he had clippings on bus protesters hurling rocks in Boston, Massachusetts; protestors in Louisville, Kentucky; and so much more

Dad was fond of his neighbors, Mr. Elton Truesdale, Mr. Bob Wright, and Mr. Jerry Clyburn. He loved his church members and his club members from the "Men's Club," and most importantly, he loved his wife and family..

Dad didn't turn anyone away regardless of race, creed, religion, or socioeconomics (rich or poor). He had such a love of God in his heart.

I remember my dad taking the time out to just be a Dad—a loving father, a supporter, and an encourager. Every now and then, he and mom would take us to the beach in one of the many station wagons we owned. We would travel to Charlotte to see our Uncle Paul, Aunt Janie, and family. We would visit his brother James and his wife Irene and family. During the summer, I remember them leaving me to stay a couple of nights. Man, I would cry to come home as soon as they would leave. Boy, I was one cry baby.

Dad always had a kind word. He loved to touch you, hug you, and reassure you that everything was going to be alright. He never gave me the impression that he was going to leave us. He loved his family with his whole heart.

From what I was told, he grew up in a stressful home. His dad was a hard factory worker and his mom, a great cook for one of the local schools. I remember to this day her delicious fried chicken and German chocolate cake! We called our grandparents, "Big Dad" and "Big Ma."

Big Dad was very strict, firm, and stern. He had temper tantrums. I was told he often abused Big Ma. There were times my dad and Big Dad would fight. Dad didn't like to see abuse; he didn't like to see his mother beaten. So, he stood up to his dad and threatened to kill him for abusing his mother. But thanks be to God, my dad didn't carry out that threat. I am grateful to God for how he changed my dad's life. As a matter of fact, they reconciled, and Big Dad became my dad's first deacon at his church in Pageland, South Carolina. God is a wonder-working God.

And if the truth be told, before my dad was a changed man, he and my mom had a couple of physical altercations as well; but obviously they had more blissful love for each other than strife. They stayed together for 60 years (from May 1, 1948 - August 2, 2008). With so many experiences in his life, he didn't mind sharing any of them. He often talked about how his life experiences made him a better person, not a bitter person.

I'm so glad my God taught my dad how to channel negative energy into positive gains. God taught him how to love instead of hate, hold grudges, or envy. No wonder his favorite scripture was **John 3:16-17,** *"For God so loved the world that He gave His only begotten Son, that whoever believes in Him should not perish but have everlasting life. For God did not send His Son into the world to condemn the world, but that the world through Him might be saved."*

He truly had a message and a mission about love in his life. He often coined a portion of the words in this old hymn, "If I could help somebody along the way; then my living shall not be in vain. If I could cheer somebody along the way, then my living shall not be in vain." His life was all about love; that's why he was able to give back to his community, his family, and to His God.

Dad was witty. He loved to laugh and make others laugh as well. He could tell the funniest jokes. I remember the one he told about the four boys: "There were four boys. One was Chinese, Mexican, white, and black. They were all sitting around bragging to see who had the better father. The Chinese man said, 'My dad was in the army; he had four stripes.' The Mexican boy said, 'My dad was in the Navy; he had three stripes.' The white boy, trying his best to top the previous stories, said, 'My dad was in the Air Force; he had one stripe.' And the black boy, who was last, of course, couldn't think of anything else to say. While scratching his head, he then belted out, 'My dad was in jail; he wore all stripes!'" I'm sure many of you reading this portion can also think of one joke Dad told. Go ahead and laugh out loud; he would!

I have to mention he had a love for sports. He was a point guard on his high

school's basketball team. I saw a picture of him standing in the middle of his team holding the ball in his 1947's Barr Street High School's annual yearbook. Man, those were the shortest shorts! And yes, he bore a wide grin.

He could shoot a mean game of pool and table tennis (ping-pong). With Dad being a crafter, he built us an original footzball (soccer) gaming system. Instead of using the traditional little men that the game is known for, Dad crafted two-inch booties that would kick the ball from place to place. Oh, what a time it was at our house when we played footzball. And when that wasn't enough, we played a good game of Spades, Bid Whist, and Rummy 500. And outside, we played Horseshoes. Dad was a great competitor! Always winning, grinning, and smiling. He was the life of our family!

Dad not only liked to sing, but dance! He had a style of his own. No one could imitate Dad's favorite dance but me. He could move from side to side with his arms raised and jerk his legs backwards. When he and mom would take the floor, we had to move aside or sit down. Those were the days!

When Dad wasn't working, he took time with each of us. He went to the PTA meetings and took us to basketball and football practices. He made sure each of us had part-time jobs, such as mowing some of our neighbors' yards, delivering newspapers, or babysitting.

Our house on Hampton Road always had something going on; it was a beacon. Many times, visitors would come by our home, known as the "Go-Get" house. It was always full from time to time with the people of the Southside. Whatever others had a need for, since Dad and Mom always had more than their share, they would aid and assist the needy with food, shelter, clothes, shoes, and money. My dad and my mom taught us all how to share, give, plant seeds, honor God, and bless others. They both were servants and missionaries from their hearts.

LOVE IS WHAT LOVE DOES

And Now These Three Remain: Faith, Hope And Love. But The Greatest of These Is Love.

THE PRAYER WARRIOR & FIGHTER
Chapter Twelve

A Celebration of Life
for
Rev. Preston and Wilma Blackmon

Saturday, May 6, 2006
2:30 P. M.

at

Pleasant Grove Baptist Church
2785 Spirit Road
Lancaster, SC 29720

Rev. Otis Lathan, Pastor

During the spring of 2006, the Lord led me to call my siblings and tell them we needed to do something for Dad and our mom. God placed it on my heart that this could possibly be the "last" celebration with his family and friends. On May 6, 2006, we made it happen at Pleasant Grove Baptist Church. We called it, "A Celebration of Life," and it was quite a celebration. We celebrated their marriage, their accomplishments, and just 'life' itself. It was a lovely occasion. It was what the Lord wanted us to do.

Six months later, Dad had an accident. He fell at the doctor's office and had to be airlifted to Carolina Medical Hospital in Charlotte, North Carolina. It was scary when I got the phone call that his brain was beginning to swell from the fall. Years ago, Dad suffered with mini-strokes from a car accident. He had many headaches and mini-strokes undetected before this fall occurred; the fall came as a result of the mini-strokes and dizziness.

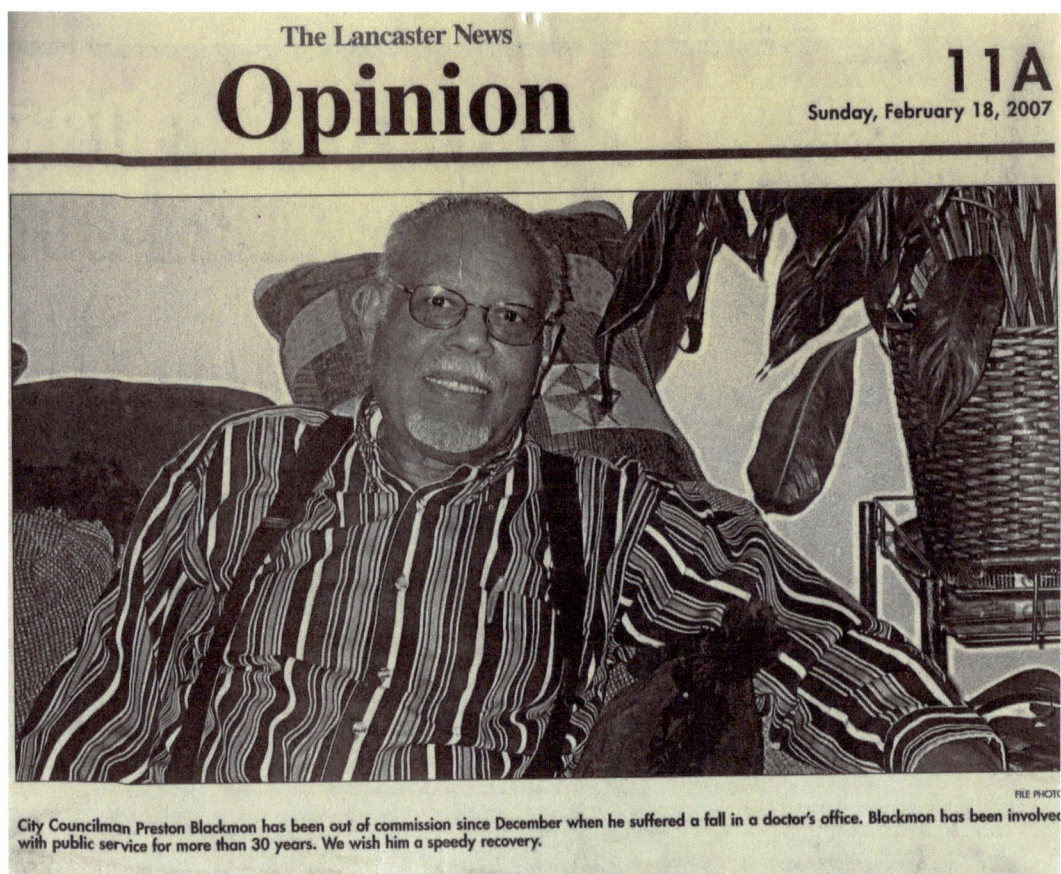

City Councilman Preston Blackmon has been out of commission since December when he suffered a fall in a doctor's office. Blackmon has been involved with public service for more than 30 years. We wish him a speedy recovery.

Being sick didn't faze Dad. He had been with the city since 1974. He meant so much to so many people who came from so many walks of life. It was hard for him to let go and let God!

He was a determined man. He was sworn in for his 10th council term at the Marion Sims Hospital, while he was in therapy and in a wheelchair.

Because of his brain injury, Dad had to have constant care. We all would take turns helping Mom to see about his needs. We all did our best to assist in any way we could. From the fall of 2006 to the summer of 2008, it was quite a challenge to see this mighty man of valor become helpless and immobile.

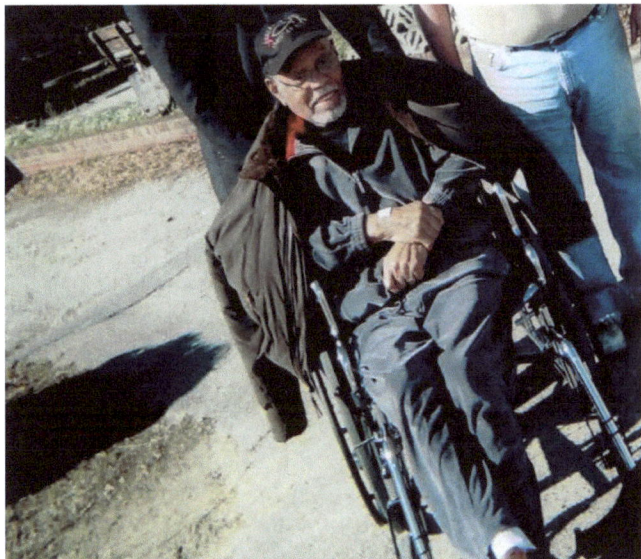

This vibrant man who was a burst of energy became silent among us. But we knew God had a purpose and a plan for everything. This was certainly a time to trust God for His promise to never leave nor forsake us **(Hebrews 13:5)**!

So many prayers were lifted throughout the community, throughout the city, and in area churches. So many pastors, friends, and leaders would stop by and pray in our home and believe God for a miracle to happen.

We all wanted Dad to walk, talk, and laugh again like before. Yet again, we had to have faith and trust God! But honestly, Dad seemed depressed. He wasn't used to sitting still all day in a wheelchair. He would get restless and would become irritable during the day. We decided to place something in his hands, anything to keep him from being bored. We placed pencils, pads, and pens in his hands, because that was his life! Something was always in his hands!

During his illness, he would constantly pull on his bed sheets or his pajamas. So, we decided to place washcloths in his hands. Then one day, about six months before he took his last breath, he shouted out, "I won't be with you all long." We all just looked at each other, as the room became quiet and still.

On August 1, 2008, minutes before he died, the nurse called my siblings and me by his bedside. We said, "It's okay, Dad, you can go now." All of a sudden, Dad's eyes opened wide. He then gave us the biggest grin, took his last breath, and went home to be with the Lord.

At 2:30 p.m., Mr. Preston, the Rev. Dr. Preston Blackmon, my dad, the father of 11 children (one deceased), and the husband of Mrs. Wilma Myers Blackmon, our Moses, went home to be with the Lord taking the Master's hand.

To my dad, a servant of all mankind, I say, "*Well done, good and faithful servant; you have been faithful over a few things, I will make you ruler over many things. Enter into the joy of your lord*" **(Matthew 25:23)**.

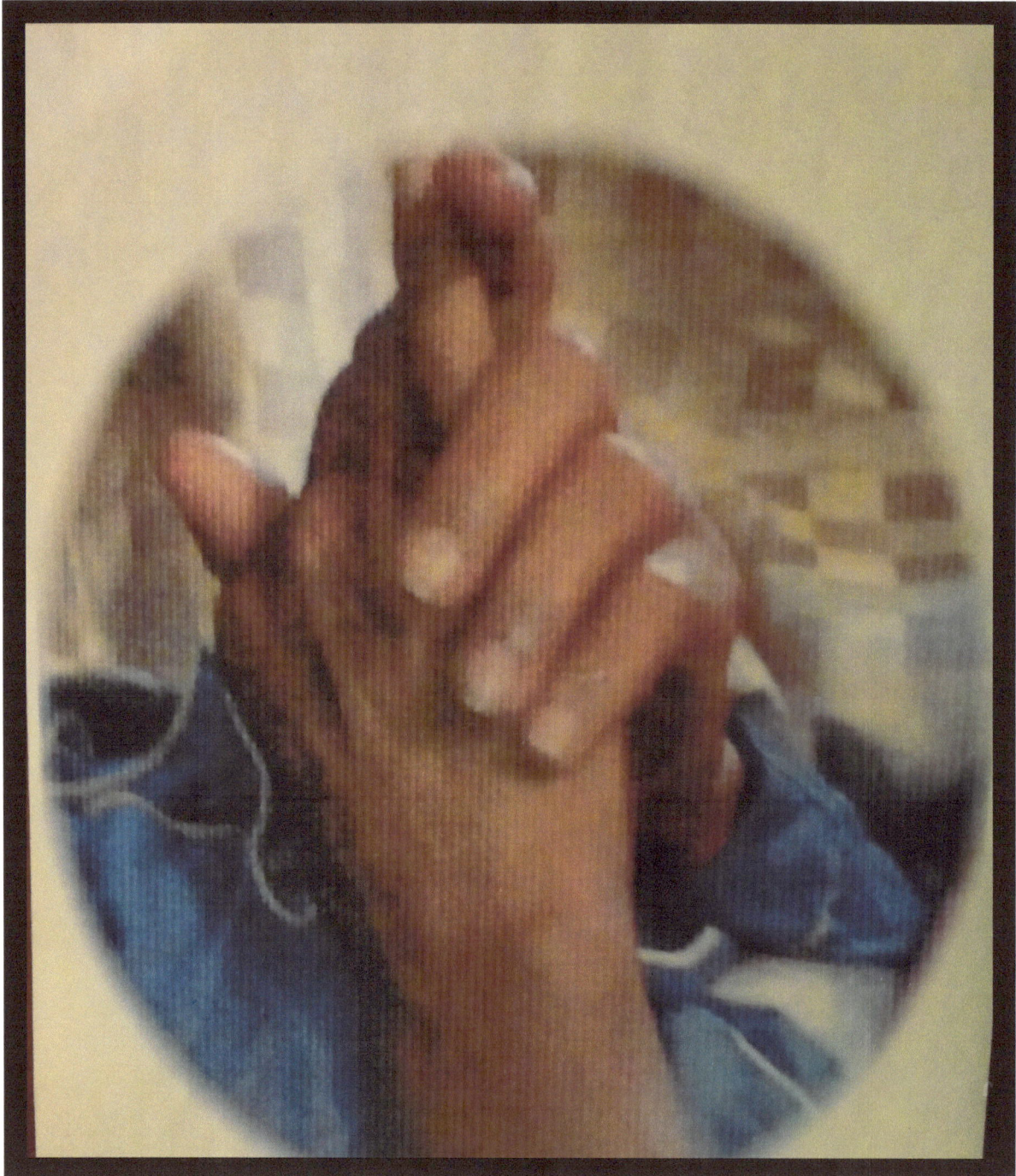

My sister Denise reminded me of the many times we would go and sing. Dad would sing lead and we would back him up. We were our own choir: Denise, Andre, Charlene, Tina, Heath, and me. His favorite was the old gospel hymn, "Packing Up." I can still hear Dad singing, as he transitioned to new Jerusalem.

I miss my dad so much. His voice is now silent, his hands are still, but his memories will live on. I can hardly wait to see him again! I thank Dad for his love, life, and legacy. The man with the mission and message, who had so much to give with his hands, is now resting from all his labors in the arms of Jesus and receiving his heavenly rewards.

It is my sincere hope, prayer, and faith that this book will be a testament of God's grace, love, and strength.

May this book forever be etched into the hearts and minds of every citizen of Lancaster and the state of South Carolina.

Well done, Dad! Your life was well-lived!

PART IV:
THE TRIBUTES

IN THE NEWS
Chapter Thirteen

City Councilman Preston Blackmon Dies
The Lancaster News
by Michele Roberts
Sunday, August 3, 2008

Lancaster County has lost a piece of history in the death of Lancaster City Councilman Preston Blackmon. He died Saturday at age 82. Blackmon served on council for 31 years, possibly making him Lancaster's longest serving councilman. He was the second black man elected to City Council.

He represented District 1 in a fair and just manner, said City Councilman Audrey Curry Jr., who represents District 3. "He was a strong advocate of justice and equality," Curry said. "He was a fair guy and he wanted to see that fairness everywhere else, too."

Curry said he, like others on council, knew of Blackmon long before they served together. Curry served with Blackmon for 17 years. "I've heard lots of stories about him, about the things he accomplished," Curry said. "From what I understand, he saw his share of injustice in earlier times and that may have been what led him into being on the council, because he thought he could make a difference in other people's lives by taking that type of position."

Blackmon, a 1947 graduate of Barr Street High School, began making his mark in Lancaster by becoming the city's first black policeman in 1959. He left that position in 1962 and went on to become not only a brick mason, but a teacher of the craft as well.

At the age of 47, Blackmon received a degree in industrial arts from S.C. State University. "He's trained a lot of craftsmen in the brick and masonry trade, but he also taught his students to conduct themselves as young men and women should," said City Councilman John Howard, who represents District 5. "That was just the way his generation was. But Preston loved helping people most of all. He was a dedicated servant for all of Lancaster's citizens."

"One of his favorite expressions was that he 'always wanted to be a bridge between all peoples and all races,'" Howard said. "Those were his exact words, and that's exactly what he tried to do."

Blackmon played an instrumental part in organizing the Southside Crime Watch, participated in a prison ministry outreach service, worked with the Southside Kidz Club and initiated the organization and construction of the Southside playground.

Blackmon also believed he was called into the ministry and after attending Atlanta Bible College, served as pastor in two churches. He also served as vice president and president of the Greater Lancaster Ministerial Association. He also served as superintendent of Sunday School and on the deacon board at First Washington Baptist Church. He was an outreach minister to the White Oak Manor nursing home and the Lancaster Rehabilitation Center.

Blackmon was very committed to his community and it showed, said County Administrator Steve Willis. "He ate, breathed and slept Lancaster," Willis said. "He might not have been the most high-profile figure, but he was actively involved in a lot of things. If he thought it would improve Lancaster, he was all for it."

"He came well-prepared to council meetings," said Lancaster Mayor Joe Shaw. "He did his homework and thought things through, and when he got there, he was ready to make a decision. He was a man of character, kindness and wisdom and he loved this city."

Blackmon was a lifetime member of the NAACP, having been a member for over 50 years and also served as the organization's third vice-president. He also served in World War II.

Blackmon was also a family man. He and his wife of 60 years, Wilma Myers Blackmon, raised 11 children, all of whom went on to receive either a college degree or advanced vocational training. From those children came 37 grandchildren and 21 great-grandchildren.

"He brought so much love and understanding of all people and all races to this city government," Shaw said. "He dedicated half of his life to help improve the quality of life for the residents of this town. He will be sorely missed."

"We are terribly sorry to lose him," Willis said. "But we should certainly thank God that he saw fit to give us Preston at all." [3]

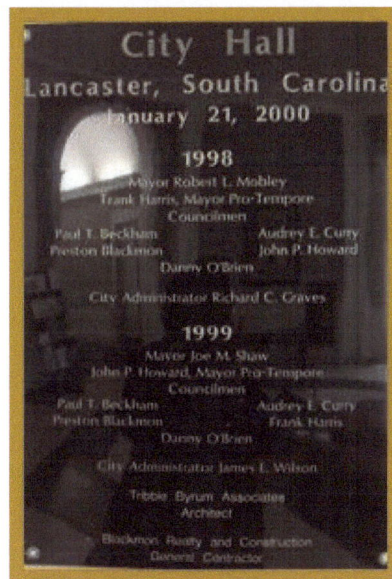

A Plaque with Dad's name hangs in City Hall along with other persons he served with from 1998 – 1999.

New Center a Testament to Legacy Left by Blackmon
The Lancaster News
by The Staff
Thursday, June 25, 2009

The late Preston Blackmon was the type of person, who once you met, quite likely you would not forget. Recently a move was made that no matter how much time passes, Blackmon's name will be honored by future generations of Lancaster County residents. Blackmon, who died last fall, was recently honored posthumously with the Preston Blackmon Family Success and Career Center in the Southside community.

The ribbon cutting was held May 15, 2009, with the open house two days later in the area of the Deliverance Word of Faith Church.

Blackmon's work in Lancaster, especially in the Southside area of the city, shows why a quality facility should bear his name. Blackmon's life is a story of success earned the old-fashioned way, the only route Blackmon knew – hard work and dedication.

His life stands as a shining example of what can be accomplished by staying on task and keeping your nose to the grindstone.

Blackmon knew reaching his goals in life meant he must be literate. His road wasn't the conventional one taken, but he reached his goal, no matter the odds. His example stands that if a goal is reachable, an individual can reach it if he is willing to do what it takes. After fulfilling a commitment to his country in the armed services, Blackmon, at age 21, returned to school and graduated from Lancaster Training School with a concentration in masonry.

After working in that field for 25 years, Blackmon pursued teacher certification as a masonry teacher and enrolled at S.C. State University.

Later on, while raising his 10 children, who each later earned specialized degrees or certification in one of two areas, Blackmon attended ministry school to become a pastor of two churches and a co-pastor of another.

"My dad believed in education and therefore took responsibility in knowing if he prepared himself, he would be the first person hired whenever an opportunity presented itself," said the Rev. Sheila Blackmon Neal, Blackmon's daughter. "He also realized education was the key to opening doors with the power to develop and mature minds beyond measure."

Blackmon proved so as he served as the first black police officer in the city of Lancaster, capably plowing future ground as a pioneer for those of his race who chose to follow that field. Blackmon proved capable and later earned a greater role as a city father on City Council.

Public service was dear to his heart and it was reflected in 34 years of making his community, city and county better.

The Preston Blackmon Family Success and Career Center stands as a monument to those who want to better themselves and improve the quality of life for others. [4]

A TRIBUTE TO MOM
Chapter Fourteen

This book will not be complete without adding my mom to this equation. She often told us, "Your dad didn't do this alone. I let him be a part of the community. He was always gone, doing things to help others. I would fix him up, dress him up, and wish him well." Then, she would say to him, "Just tell those women out there, you are coming back home."

Being a homemaker with 10 children to raise, Mom kept us, Dad, the house, and herself. She enjoyed serving her household. Each morning, when we were little, she served pans and pans of hot biscuits.

She didn't leave the home very often. She would say, "Who was going to keep a house full of kids?" My mom possesses such humility; she's so loving and giving. God gave her the heart of a servant. And she loved it! It gave her joy to share what she had. She once said, "God entrusted her to give to the poor, to reach out to the needy, and to set at liberty the captive and the brokenhearted." She would often utter the words (while setting them to a melodic tune), "I am a living testimony. I'm in the Lord's hands. He's taking care of me." And He has.

On January 15, 2019, Mom turned 89 years old. We celebrated her life and her love. I have the greatest mom any child could ever ask for. She never let us want for anything. If it was in her power to do it, she did it. And she did it well.

She once worked in my uncle's establishment in the Southside Community and at Mungo Funeral Home fixing the hair of the deceased.

She also cooked and baked for Barr Street High School in Lancaster, South Carolina. And before she retired, she became a licensed home-health certified nurse; she occupied that position for 18 years before she retired.

Along with Dad, Mom served as a missionary in the community, providing the needy and bereaved with clothing, shelter, and food. Not only was she a great helpmate for my dad, a great mother to my siblings and me, but she was also a pillar of strength for our community.

Mom's outstanding commitments were:

- Volunteer Hospital Auxiliary at Marion Sims Hospital – 300 hours (Lancaster, SC)
- Volunteer Hope Center – 14 years (Lancaster, SC)
- Member of the Southside Socialite Club
- Eastern Star Lodge Member, Queen Elizabeth # 179 - 50 years (Lifetime Membership Certificate)

Mom was the recipient of the following prestigious awards:

- Humanity Award, "Woman as the Lights of Tomorrow"
- Community Service Award, Omega Psi Phi Fraternity, Inc. (November 22, 2009)
- Unsung Hero Appreciation Award, Southside Adult Family Literacy Project (February 25, 2010)

Arise! Ye Daughters of Zion

Arise! ye daughter of Zion! March! Be Steadfast! Take your place! You have work to do; God is depending on you.

Arise! Ye Daughter of Zion! Remember your grandmother, the midwives, your mother; remember their struggles and their tears.

Arise! Ye Daughter of Zion! From slavery, to the underground railroad, to the cotton fields of yesteryears!

Arise! Ye Daughter of Zion! From being depressed and rejected, from being misused and disrespected, from being raped, used, and abused.

Arise! From raising your own sisters and brothers to single motherhood;

Arise! From all these disparities to hope, peace, joy, and love that only God can give; not man!

Arise! From depending on resources that one day cannot and will not exist; educate yourself and breathe hope into your being to ensure opportunities, liberty, and blessings to come;

Arise! From the depths of Harriet Tubman, Rosa Parks, and Shirley Chisolm;

Arise! From the tracks of Wilma Rudolph, Madame C.J. Walker, and Mary Mcleod Bethune.

Arise! From the cures of Edmonia Lewis, Joan of Arc, and Betty Shabazz;

Arise! From the paths and shadows of deceased women of this church (the Mount Zion Church) who labored tirelessly in the vineyard;

Arise! Ye daughter of Zion! From all of your struggles to ultimate strengths.

We need your wisdom to teach and not to discourage.
We need your hands to mend and not to tear down.
We need your compassion to heal and not to hurt.
We need your dreams to inspire and not to condemn.
We need your talents to cultivate and not to neglect.
We need your boldness to lead and not to be ashamed.
We need your faith to initiate prayers and not to doubt.

Arise! Ye daughter of Zion! We need your love to unify this church as one in Christ!

Arise! God needs you;

Arise! Ye daughter of Zion!

March! Be Steadfast! Take your place! You have work to do;

God is depending on you.

I love you mother; your third daughter, Sheila.

~ Sheila Blackmon-Neal
April 13, 2000

Dedicated to Wilma Myers Blackmon

Praise the Lord! I'm Free!

Wilma M. Blackmon

January 15, 1930 - June 9, 2020

Back in love again!

FINAL TRIBUTE
Chapter Fifteen

"GOD, SEND US MEN"

God, send us men who will stand and not fall.
God, send us men who can withstand it all.
God, send us men who will not give up or give in.
God, send us men who will be prepared to win.

God, send us men who will honor your Word.
God, send us men who are not afraid to be heard.
God, send us men who are not ashamed to lead.
God, send us men who will help to meet others' needs.

God, you sent us David, a strong and courageous man.
God, you sent us Moses, with a rod in his hand.
God, you sent us Paul, who preached across the land.
God, you sent us Jesus, the Son of God and man.

God, hear my prayer; we need men to care!

We need leaders, teachers, ministers, and preachers.
Men who build with wisdom and skill.
Judges, doctors, pilots, and cooks;
We need men who will live by the "good" book.

Oh Lord, we thank you for Malcolm, Martin, Jesse, and George.
We thank you for Colin, Benjamin, Jackson, and Medgar.
We thank you for Crispus, Fredrick, and William.
We thank you for those men who carried many banners.

Lord, lest we forget those fathers who stayed with their wives and children and saw a
need to keep food on the table, clothes on everyone's back, and shelter from the rain.
Lord, keep our men in your prayers; give them faith, patience, and hope to know
it was you all the time who brought them through their pain.

Now, Lord, after you have considered all these things, give us pure love that only you
can bring.
Thank you, Lord, for hearing my prayer.
Send us, dear Jesus, men who care.

~ Sheila Blackmon-Neal - June 12, 1999

A LETTER TO DAD
Chapter Sixteen

If I had to thank Dad on behalf of all of my brothers and sisters, I would probably say something like this...

Dear Dad,

If I were **Krystal**, *I would thank you for:*
- giving me life.
- remembering me when others forgot me.
- giving me my sense of humor.
- loving, embracing, and accepting me after we met for the first time after twenty-three years.
- giving me hope to go on. Love you, Dad!

If I were **Derrall**, *I would thank you for:*

- encouraging me to play my snare drum. And for all the times you waved at me in the annual parade on Main Street.
- allowing me to be your oldest son and for giving me your name.
- showing me how to work hard, knowing this was the only way to have anything in life.
- praying for me day and night as I tried to cope with everyday life as a young soldier in Da Nang, Vietnam.
- always being there. Love you, Pops!

If I were **Ricardo-Rickey**, *I would thank you for:*

- beating me and disciplining me for climbing trees, throwing rocks, swearing, and cursing as a "little-mouthy" boy.
- listening to me as I blew my trumpet and saw your smile of approval.
- calling and checking on me when you moved to Aiken County to work, especially the time when I almost lost my ring finger.
- showing me how to have a love and respect for automobiles.
- coming to Fort Benning, Georgia. I was a soldier there, wrongly accused, and

I needed your strength, faith, and courage to help me make it through. I am eternally grateful!

If I were **Denise**, *I would thank you for:*

- spoiling me rotten! I am still in your heart; and you will always be mine.
- praying with me in faith that God would heal my scarlet fever.
- all your support when I was in school.
- being there when my first son Rico was born.
- coming to my college graduation.
- protecting me from all the *"wolves"* (the boys) in the neighborhood who wanted to devour me. You stood up for me! Now I understand that you only wanted what was best for me.

If I were **Andre**, *I would thank you for:*

- visiting me at Fort Jackson when I knew some things I did you were not proud, but you loved me in spite of.
- housing my wife, children, and me.
- giving me sound advice, even though, many times I didn't want to hear it. Thanks, Dad! You knew what was best for me.
- coming to the hospital when I was at the point of death.
- showing me how to drive a school bus.
- supporting me when I caused an accident with a young child.
- Helping me through the hard times I had in Kentucky. Thanks for telling me that God cares.

If I were **Charlene**, *I would thank you for:*

- being there when I broke my arm, when my gums were knocked loose, when I got hit in the head with a baseball bat, and when I was involved in several car accidents. I'm sorry, Dad, that I was your accident-prone child.
- watching me march with my flute on the Marching 101 Band at South Carolina State University. You looked so proud of me!
- helping me raise my children with godly advice.

- visiting me from one hospital to another, some 20 odd times.

If I were **Ada**, *I would thank you for:*

- giving me your mom's name (Ada) and yours (Prestina). I am doubly-blessed.
- all the beatings I got for running my mouth. I was only mimicking you.
- showing me how to fix and repair pipes, bicycles, roofs, engines, commodes, and God knows what else.
- praying that God would shield and protect me while I resided in the city of New York.
- trusting me with your financial affairs, while demonstrating to me work and business ethics.

If I were **Laritz**, *I would thank you for:*

- my beautiful locks of hair and handsome looks.
- giving me life and releasing me into the bosom of Jesus, knowing that God had a better plan for me.

If I were **Heath**, *I would thank you for:*

- buying so many Tonka trucks after I tore up so many others.
- screaming, *"Run, Heath, run"* on the football field. I was the only son that played sports like you.
- teaching me dignity, respect, and honor as a soldier.
- supporting my tutor instructor, so I could become an accomplished reader.
- praying and believing God would heal me from bronchitis.

If I were **Onatha (Shawn)**, *I would thank you for:*

- not giving up on me when I wanted to give up on myself.
- sending me to beauty school in Sumter, South Carolina.
- letting me drive my own car, The Pinto!
- allowing me to be your baby daughter; you saved the best for last.
- helping me raise my children and loving my husband John as your own son.

Last, but not least, **I** *want to thank you for:*

- delivering me on July 11, 1958 after 7:00 p.m.
- allowing me to be the neighborhood's tomboy; I was the best quarterback, basketball player, newspaper carrier, babysitter, and lawn cutter. All of this helped me raise my son, Samuel, practically by myself.
- allowing me to sing with you in the family choir. A lot of those songs I didn't know, but I tried. Those songs you sang are giving me a witness NOW of how good God is. Songs like, "I Found Him," "Packing Up," and "God is Real."
- coming to my sixth-grade class when I was so stressed from prejudiced classmates. I knew you were praying for me.
- calling on the name of Jesus when I nearly drowned in a lake.
- showing me how to pack my artwork, my frames, and my paintings as we hauled them in the station wagon going from point A to point B.
- all the counsel and advice you gave me. For telling me, "To whom much is given, much is required" (**Luke 12:48**). At the time, I didn't know this was a scripture from the Holy Bible. You were talking about all the gifts God bestowed upon me. Now I know that I am favored by God.
- sharing your artistic skills, teaching abilities (not knowing I was going to be a teacher just like you), and the gift of love.

And in closing this letter, what else can I say as I watch your once strengthened body become frail from your accident in November 2006? All I can say is, I am so proud of you. Rest from all of your labors. Trust God to carry you through this valley of sickness and pain. Hold fast to your confession of faith. Just know that everything is going to be alright.

Love,

Your daughter, Sheila (a.k.a. Red)
February 15, 2007
(three months after Dad's accident)

SPECIAL TRIBUTES
Chapter Seventeen

Tribute 1

As a child and young teenager, my mother, Delores Blackmon, would send my brother (Raymond) and me to Lancaster to stay for the summer with Papa and Grandma.

During my summer vacations, I would be expecting just that, vacation! "NOT in Papa's House!" When he got up, we all got up! He would take Uncle Heath and me out with him on his jobs as a brick mason. I was his junior apprentice/helper. At the time, I was barely 100 pounds and I was carrying bricks and mixing cement.

I grew up in the city life; so I was used to doing household chores and playing basketball all day…NOT moving bricks! It felt like slavery at the time, but I learned that hard work, as well as learning a skill is important.

Papa was my Superman; there was nothing my Papa couldn't fix, try to fix, or achieve in life. He would try anything and wouldn't stop until he accomplished his mission.

Papa was a father, grandfather, husband, pastor, brick mason, World War II veteran, policeman, barber, councilman (and the list continues); he taught me so much. He showed so much love and discipline. He showed me how a man is supposed to provide and protect his family. He taught me how to stand my ground and demand respect in everything I do. His respect came from how much love he showed his family and community.

The last memorable touching moment I had with Papa was when I came to Lancaster for a long weekend to check on him, because he had fallen at the doctor's office. I made a last-minute drive and popped up at his home. He was doing well and delighted to see me. He called me "New York." He said, "New York came to see me!"

As we all sat around and talked for a while, he realized it was my birthday. Papa stated that had he known he would have gotten me a cake or something. I told him, "I appreciate the thought, but I'm okay." Shortly thereafter, he went into the kitchen messing around with stuff. Grandma asked, "What are you doing?" He said, "Nothing!"

Moments later, he came out of the kitchen. And there, to my surprise, he placed a pack of Twinkies on a plate with a bright candle stuck in the middle, singing "Happy Birthday" to me. Just writing this brings happy tears to my eyes.

Soon after, Papa started going down from his injury.

Every Black History Month, I celebrate my grandfather; he's my inspiration. He is and was "SOUTHSIDE!!"

With lots of Love Papa,
Your Oldest Grandson, Ricardo Lazarus Blackmon

Tribute 2

Although they had 11 children of their own, Preston and Wilma Blackmon were parents to EVERYBODY!!! They both personally saw me through some very difficult times, but there is one special incident that I remember Rev. Preston Blackmon for (my nickname for him was "Grandpop") and that was my graduation from the University of South Carolina. Grandpop surprised me by coming to my graduation when I received my Master's degree in Social Work in 1985.

My own father, Bill Gordon, passed away in 1978, and I received my BA degree in Psychology in 1983 (also from USC). I was so shocked to see him and especially so when he said, "I had to come because I had to stand in for your father since he could not be here on this special occasion." I will NEVER forget his kindness & thoughtfulness for being with my family & me on that special day.

Ms. Brenda Gordon Pogue

Vote
PRESTON
BLACKMON

CITY COUNCIL
"A Man You Can Trust"

YOUR SUPPORT & VOTE
WILL BE APPRECIATED

COUNCILMAN & MRS. PRESTON BLACKMON & FAMILY

Congratulations
For Me and My House, We Will Keep the Dream ALIVE.

A look back

Preston Blackmon, Lancaster city councilman, and his wife, Wilma, were a pa[...] fashion scene in 1948 in Lancaster. (*Photo courtesy of Ada Blackmon.*)

Councilman upset over loan fund restrictions

Fund can only be used for some home repairs

BY JOHNATHAN C. RYAN
STAFF WRITER

Lancaster City Councilman Preston Blackmon appeared irked Tuesday night after learning of restrictions on a $130,000 fund for home-improvement loans or grants in the Southside area.

The money is available to qualifying homeowners, mainly in Blackmon's district. It comes from a revolving loan fund started in the mid-1980s by the federal government.

Lancaster City Administrator Steve Willis told council Tuesday that S.C. Department of Commerce officials have indicated the money can be used for emergency repairs after a tornado, flood or fire, but not for repairs, such as a new roof or heater.

Blackmon

In January, council asked Willis to find out whether such repairs would qualify under fund guidelines. The city also sought to extend the target area beyond the Southside neighborhood, but Willis said doing so would require environmental studies and surveys, which would cost more than is in the fund.

There's always "nine or 10 reasons why the money shouldn't be used," Blackmon said.

See FUND, Page 2A

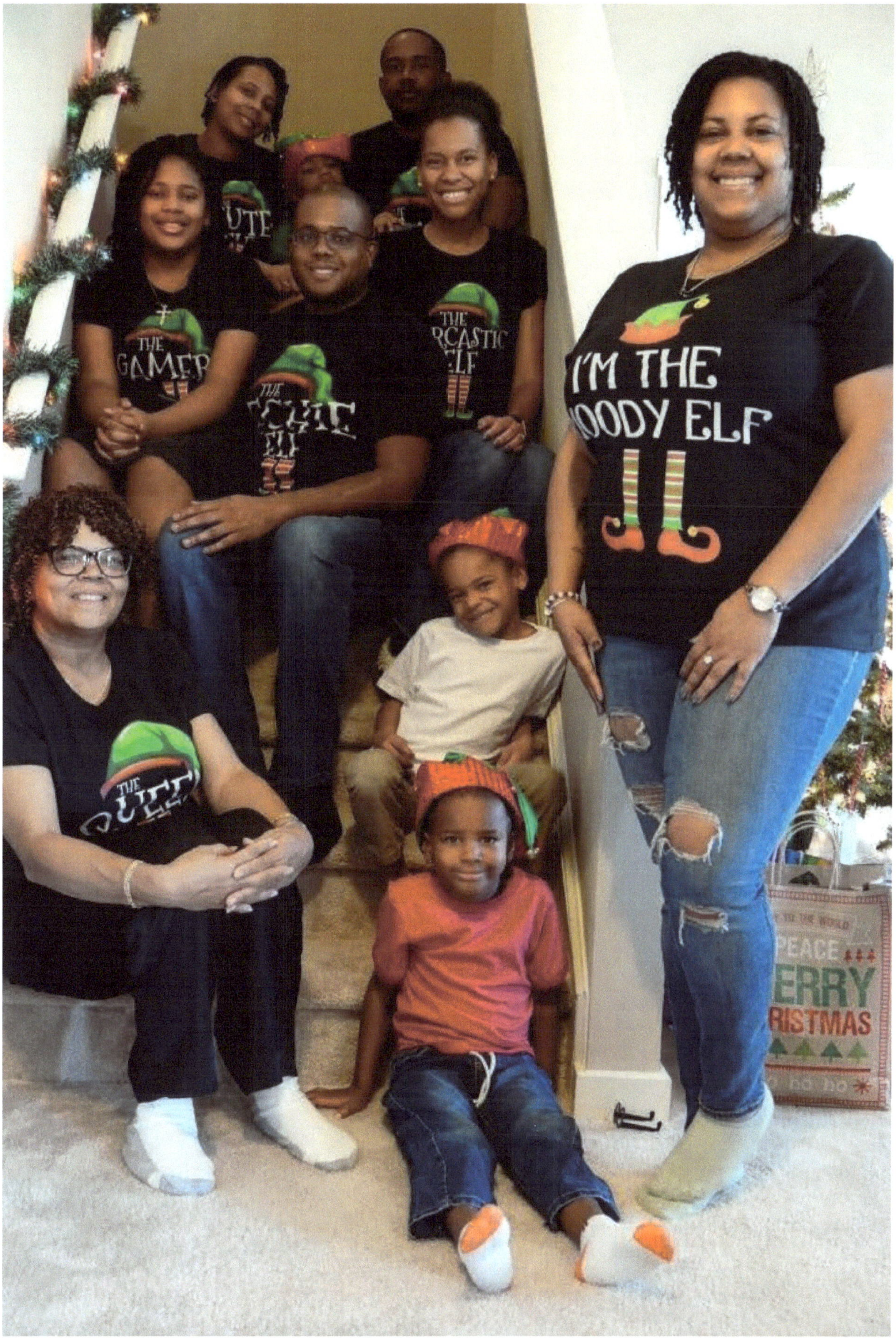
THE GAMER
I'M THE
PEACE

Certificate of Recognition

Preston Blackmon

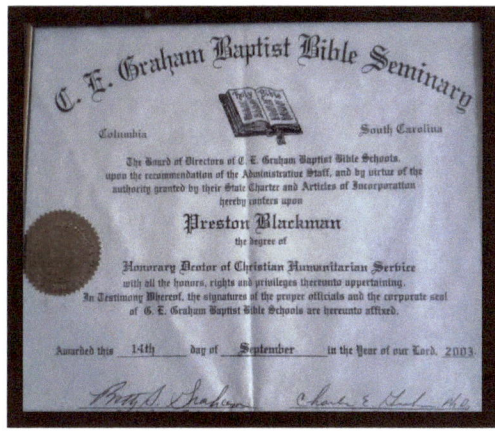

C. E. Graham Baptist Bible Seminary

Columbia   South Carolina

Preston Blackman

the degree of

Honorary Doctor of Christian Humanitarian Service

Awarded this 14th day of September in the Year of our Lord 2003

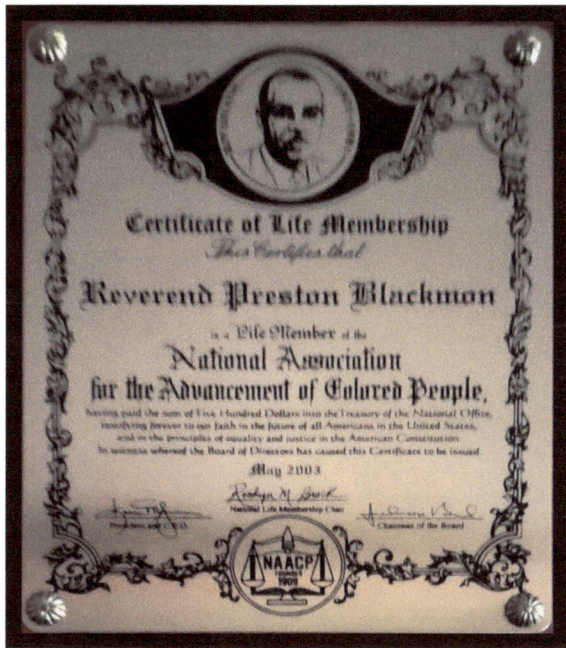

Certificate of Life Membership

This Certifies that

Reverend Preston Blackmon

is a Life Member of the

National Association for the Advancement of Colored People,

May 2003

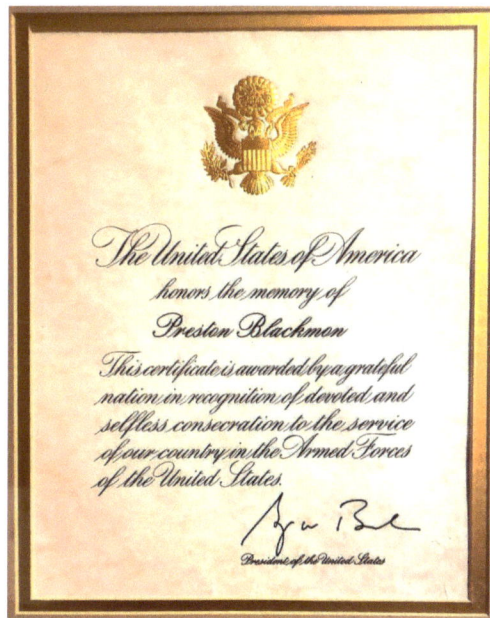

The United States of America

honors the memory of

Preston Blackmon

This certificate is awarded by a grateful nation in recognition of devoted and selfless consecration to the service of our country in the Armed Forces of the United States.

President of the United States

Petition
TO THE
Congress of the United States

CONFIRMED TO:
Mr Preston Blackmon
420 Hampton Rd
Lancaster, SC 29720

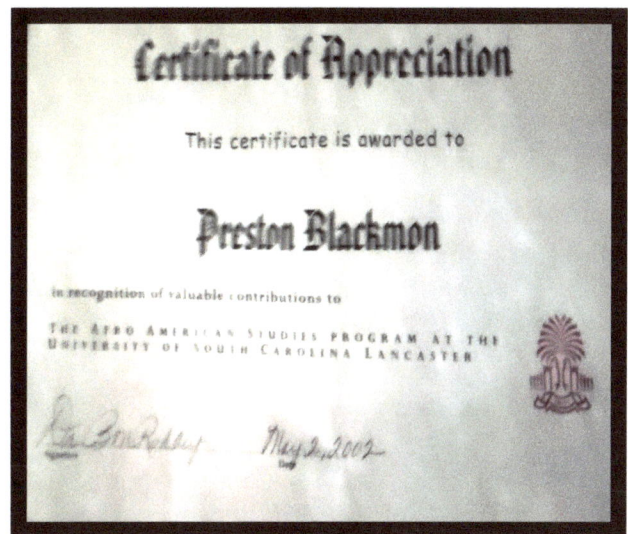

Certificate of Appreciation

This certificate is awarded to

Preston Blackmon

in recognition of valuable contributions to

THE AFRO AMERICAN STUDIES PROGRAM AT THE
UNIVERSITY OF SOUTH CAROLINA LANCASTER

May 2, 2002

Preston Stands For:

Pillar of strength for his family
Religious believer
Energetic and bold soldier
Singer, artist, inventor
Teacher & Counselor
Overcomer of adversity
Never gave up; never looked back

~ Sheila Blackmon-Neal

I didn't realize that my dad and I had so much in common until this book was completed. We both taught school, preached the gospel, and sang on many choirs. Like my dad, I love to read and purchase books; draw and paint; create and design. We both understood that we should love people, but hate injustice. I've been told that I look like him, walk like him, and talk like him. I have his skinny legs, dry feet, and even his bald head! I can't deny, he's my dad.

Paul wrote in **Philippians 3:12-14**: *12 Not that I have already attained, or am already perfected; but I press on, that I may lay hold of that for which Christ Jesus has also laid hold of me. 13 Brethren, I do not count myself to have apprehended; but one thing I do, forgetting those things which are behind and reaching forward to those things which are ahead, 14 I press toward the goal for the prize of the upward call of God in Christ Jesus.*

My dad "fought a good fight, he finished his course, and he kept the faith" (**2 Timothy 4:7**). I thank God he gained the victory. I can hardly wait to see his face and broad smile again. Until then, it is my hope, faith, and prayer that his seeds will further his love, life, and legacy until we all meet again.

ABOUT THE AUTHOR

Rev. Sheila Blackmon-Neal was born the seventh child of the late Rev. Dr. Preston and Wilma Myers Blackmon. She is the widow of the late Deacon William G. Neal.

After graduating from Lancaster High School in Lancaster, SC, in 1975, she enrolled at Allen University, majoring in Art Education. In the fall of 1977, she transferred to South Carolina State University in Orangeburg, SC, and graduated with a Bachelor's degree in Art Education in the fall of December 1980. In 1998, she earned a Master's of Education degree in Educational Leadership from Cambridge College in Cambridge, Massachusetts.

She is a retired teacher, having taught for 32 years in Williamsburg County and Sumter County, with God's blessing.

God has blessed her with so many gifts. Art and music were always her passion as a young child. She also loved to write songs, plays, skits, and poetry throughout her life. She is grateful to God, and she gives him continual praise, glory, and honor.

In the year of 2000, God called her into the ministry to preach the gospel. After the call of God was so heavy on her heart, she enrolled at Beacon University (Macon, Georgia) and completed her Master's degree in Divinity and Theology in 2007. She is presently a full-time pastor of the One Step Christian Ministries in Bishopville, South Carolina.

Rev. Sheila Blackmon-Neal is also the author of a children's book that pays homage to her father entitled *What's In Your Hand, Mr. Preston?*

REFERENCES

1 City of Lancaster SC. (2017). History of Lancaster. Retrieved from https://www.lancastercitysc.com/history-of-lancaster/

2 Wikipedia. Lancaster, South Carolina. Retrieved from https://en.wikipedia.org/wiki/Lancaster,_South_Carolina

3 Roberts, M. (2008, August 3). City Councilman Preston Blackmon Dies. The Lancaster News. Retrieved from https://www.thelancasternews.com/content/city-councilman-preston-blackmon-dies

4 The Staff. (2009, June 25). New Center a Testament to Legacy Left by Blackmon. The Lancaster News. Retrieved from https://www.thelancasternews.com/content/new-center-testament-legacy-left-blackmon